W0037805

Best Dressed Pets

A Sticker & Colouring Book

Nicole Jarecz & Lisa Regan

Published in 2015 by Laurence King Publishing Ltd,
361–373 City Road, London EC1V 1LR, United Kingdom
Tel: + 44 20 7841 6900, Fax: + 44 20 7841 6910,
e-mail: enquiries@laurenceking.com, www.laurenceking.com

Copyright © illustrations 2014 Nicole Jarecz
Text and research by Lisa Regan

All rights reserved. No part of this publication may be reproduced or transmitted in any form
or by any means, electronic or mechanical, including photocopy, recording, or any information
storage and retrieval system, without prior permission in writing from the publisher.

A catalogue record for this book is available from the British Library.

ISBN: 978 1 78067 474 2

Design: Eleanor Ridsdale
Printed in Malaysia

Surf style

The sun's out, the surf is up, and your pooches can't wait to feel the sand between their claws! For you, the choice is simple: bikini or swimsuit? Add a cute cover-up, a floppy hat and lots of sunscreen and you're good to go. For your beach bow-wow, there are so many things to remember: bandana, collar, towel, lead, water bowl… all perfectly coordinated, of course!!

Purr-fect party

Who says that only you should have fun in the party season? Take your beautifully behaved best friends along, they love an excuse to dress up! Put on your best outfit, glam-up your hair, and give your pets some preening. They'll be the guests of honour, for sure! (Just keep them away from the canapés…)

Thirsty work

Catch up on the gossip with a girlie outing! You can show off your new outfit, get some fresh air, and take your pet pooch for a walk, all at the same time. Dogs are sociable animals so they love to get out and about and sniff out some furry friends. Make sure they're accessorized to the max – you never know who you might bump into!

Let sleeping dogs lie!

Invite the girls for a sleepover, and make sure they bring their pets along. Who needs a teddy bear when you have a huggable hound to cuddle up to? Everything should be fluffy at bedtime – your PJs, your slippers, and definitely your four-legged friends!

Garden party

Ah, time to relax in the sunshine! Slip into something cool and comfy and pour yourself an ice-cold drink to enjoy on the patio. Play with prints and patterns for your summer clothes, and keep the shapes loose and flowing for when the temperature rises. Your darling doggies can have fun in the sun, too, and won't mind you dressing them in the brightest shirts at the party!

COUNTRY CASUAL

Animal lovers know that looking their best sometimes has to mix with the demands of pet care. Put away your party dress and sling on some stable wear – practical, comfortable, washable but still delectable. Make mucking out more fun with a friend to help, plus your faithful pets to keep you company. Just don't expect the glamour puss to get her paws dirty!

Surf style

LIFE IS A ❤ A BEACH

Purr-fect party

Thirsty work

Let sleeping dogs lie!

Garden party

COUNTRY CASUAL

WATCHING THE
WORLD GO BY

True blue

STREET LIFE

Winter warmers

Best
dressed

Let's fly a kite

WATCHING THE WORLD GO BY

Show that you're street-savvy when walking the dogs, with tough-girl boots and sports-chic clothes. It doesn't matter if your canine friend is a real big softie – that just goes to show, you can't judge personality by the clothes being worn!

True blue

What's the only thing that's as great as denim? More denim, of course!
Go to town with varying shades, shapes and styles. Dress up your jeans
with a denim blazer, or dress right down with dungarees. This is one
trend your pup can carry off from season to season – dogs do double
denim with puppy panache!

STREET LIFE

Whether you're window-shopping or hoping to bag a bargain, it's good to know you're looking your best. Stay ahead of the rest with city chic – it's all about being smart, stylish and feeling confident about your clothes. Add some understated accessories, and make sure your dog is dressed to impress, too!

Winter warmers

Baby, it's cold outside! But don't stay caged up indoors. Wrap up warm and head out to play – your pup will love it! Jump around and join in the fun and you'll soon forget about the cold. Plus, dogs in sweaters are just adorable, and you can coordinate your knits for some super-fun fashion!

Best dressed

Take your pets to prom night! Give your favourite animals the red-carpet treatment and make them feel like a million dollars – diamonds are a cat's best friend, too! Go for all-out glamour yourself, with statement hemlines, eye-catching colours, luxurious fabrics, and as much bling as you like…

Let's fly a kite

Put some wind in your sails and brave the elements! Outdoors fashions are great fun, for you and your furry friends – go with cosy knits, chunky boots, and lots of layers. Flying a kite or chasing sticks will keep you and your hound happy, and help to blow away the cobwebs.

What to wear?

It's so tricky deciding what to wear! Especially if you're invited to a top notch fashion event – the pressure is on… Choose your favourite outfit and add accessories that really make it pop!